THE SELF-HELP HANDBOOK: A COMPREHENSIVE GUIDE

25+ BOOK SUMMARIES FROM SELF-HELP AUTHORS AROUND THE WORLD!

KRISHIV NEGI

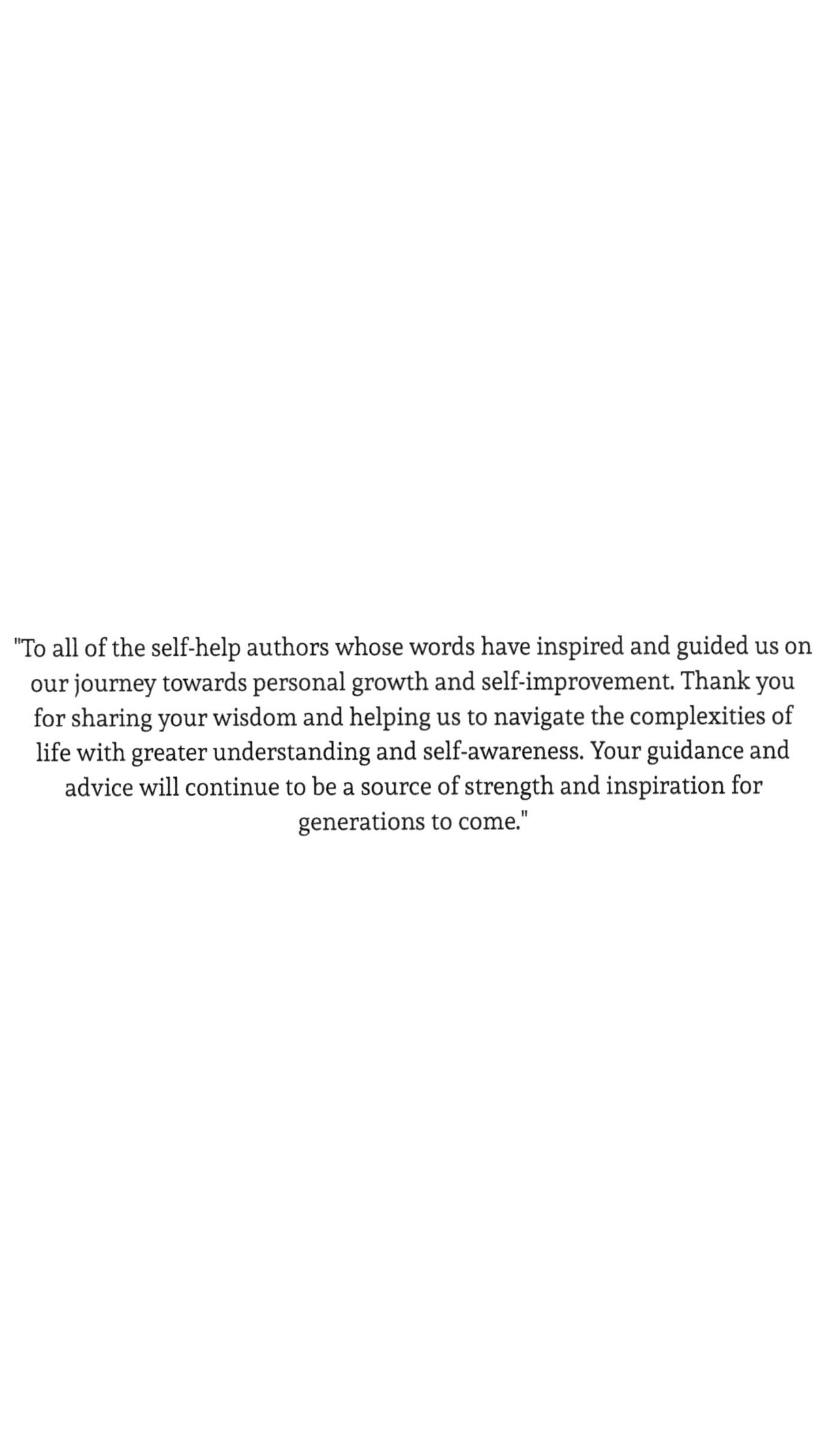

"To all of the self-help authors whose words have inspired and guided us on our journey towards personal growth and self-improvement. Thank you for sharing your wisdom and helping us to navigate the complexities of life with greater understanding and self-awareness. Your guidance and advice will continue to be a source of strength and inspiration for generations to come."

Contents

Contents

Foreword

" I am honored to write the foreword for this unique and valuable resource. This book brings together the wisdom and insights of some of the world's most respected self-help authors, providing a comprehensive overview of the key concepts and ideas that have shaped the genre. Whether you are new to the world of self-help or are a seasoned reader seeking to deepen your understanding, this book offers something for everyone. I highly recommend it to anyone looking to make positive changes in their life and to live to their full potential."

Preface

As the author of this book, I am thrilled to have the opportunity to share with you the insights and wisdom of some of the world's most respected self-help authors. When I first embarked on my journey of personal growth and self-improvement, I was overwhelmed by the sheer number of books and resources available. It was difficult to know where to start and how to discern the truly valuable information from the noise.

That's why I decided to create this book - to provide a comprehensive overview of the key ideas and concepts from the self-help genre, all in one place. Through careful selection and summarization, I have distilled the essence of dozens of books into a single, easy-to-digest volume.

Whether you are just starting out on your self-improvement journey or are looking to deepen your understanding of the field, this book is for you. Inside, you will find the insights and advice of some of the most successful and influential self-help authors of all time, covering a wide range of topics including goal-setting, time management, mindfulness, relationships, and much more.

For my two all time favourite book by Dale Carnegie How to win friends and influence people, I have included takeaways from all the chapters.

I hope that this book will serve as a valuable resource for you, providing guidance and inspiration on your path towards personal growth and self-improvement. Thank you for choosing to join me on this journey.

Acknowledgements

I would like to express my sincere gratitude to all of the self-help authors whose works are featured in this book. Your wisdom and insights have been an invaluable source of inspiration and guidance for me, and I am honored to have the opportunity to share them with others.

I would also like to thank my family and friends for their love and support throughout the reading and writing process. Their encouragement and belief in me have been a constant source of strength and motivation.

Finally, I would like to extend my appreciation to my publisher for their guidance and expertise in bringing this project to fruition. It is with their help that this book has become a reality.

Thank you all for your contributions to this project. It is with great pleasure that I present to you this summary of self-help books from some of the most brilliant and compassionate minds in the world."

Short Story

Here is a short story on self-improvements and its benefits.

It was a typical Monday morning, and Rachel was feeling overwhelmed as she sat at her desk, staring at her to-do list. She had a lot on her plate at work, and she felt like she was always falling behind. She was also struggling with her self-confidence, feeling like she wasn't good enough and like she was always making mistakes.

As she sat there, feeling frustrated and stuck, she decided that enough was enough. She was tired of feeling overwhelmed and inadequate, and she was determined to make a change. She knew that if she wanted to feel better about herself and be more successful, she would have to work on improving herself.

So, she started by making a plan. She identified the areas of her life that she wanted to work on – her work habits, her health, and her relationships – and she set specific, achievable goals for each of these areas.

First, Rachel focused on improving her work habits. She made a schedule for herself, breaking her tasks down into smaller, more manageable chunks. She also started getting up earlier in the morning, so that she could get a jump start on her day. This helped her to feel more organized and in control of her time, and she started making progress on her to-do list.

Next, Rachel turned her attention to her health. She knew that she needed to take better care of herself if she wanted to feel better and be more productive. So, she started exercising regularly and eating a healthier diet. She also made an effort to get enough sleep, which helped her to feel more energetic and focused.

Finally, Rachel worked on improving her relationships. She made an effort to be more understanding and supportive of her friends and family, and she tried to be more open and honest with them about her feelings. She also made an effort to be more present in her relationships, rather than always being distracted by work or other commitments.

As Rachel worked on improving herself, she started to see some real progress. She felt more confident and capable at work, and she was making more of an impact in her job. She also felt healthier and more energetic, and she was able to enjoy her relationships more.

As Rachel continued on her journey of self-improvement, she started to notice some other benefits as well. She was more productive at work, and she was getting more done in less time. She also started to feel more confident in herself and her abilities, and she was no longer as prone to feeling overwhelmed or stressed out.

One of the biggest changes Rachel noticed was in her relationships. She had always struggled to be open and honest with people, but as she worked on being more present and understanding, she found that her relationships became stronger and more meaningful. She was able to connect with people on a deeper level, and she found that she was more able to support and encourage others.

Rachel also started to feel more fulfilled and satisfied with her life overall. She had always felt like something was missing, but as she worked on improving herself, she realized that the missing piece was within her all along. She was able to find her passion and purpose, and she felt more motivated and driven to pursue her goals.

Despite all of the progress she had made, Rachel knew that she still had a long way to go. She was constantly learning and growing, and she knew that there would always be more challenges and obstacles to overcome. But she was up for the challenge, and she was determined to keep working on herself, no matter what.

As she looked back on the journey she had been on, Rachel couldn't believe how far she had come. She had come a long way from feeling overwhelmed and stuck, and she was grateful for everything she had learned and experienced along the way. She knew that the road ahead would be full of ups and downs, but she was ready for whatever came her way. She was confident in herself and her abilities, and she knew that she had the grit and determination to do the epic shit and make the impossible possible.

As Rachel continued on her journey of self-improvement, she started to realize the value of self-help books. She had always been skeptical of these kinds of books, thinking that they were a bit of a scam and that they wouldn't really be able to help her. But as she started reading more and more of them, she found that they were actually incredibly useful.

One of the benefits that Rachel got from reading self-help books was a new perspective on her problems. She had always thought of her struggles as being unique to her, and she had felt alone and misunderstood. But as she read the stories and advice of others who had faced similar challenges, she realized that she wasn't alone at all. She saw that there were people out there who understood what she was going through, and she felt more connected and supported as a result.

Another benefit of self-help books for Rachel was the practical advice and tools that they provided. She found that many of the books she read had concrete steps and exercises that she could follow to help her work through her issues and make positive changes in her life. She found that these tools were particularly helpful when it came to things like setting goals, overcoming negative thought patterns, and developing healthy habits.

In addition to all of these benefits, Rachel also found that reading self-help books was simply enjoyable. She had always loved to read, and she found that these kinds of books were inspiring and motivating in a way that other books weren't. She loved the feeling of accomplishment that came with finishing a book, and she found that she was always eager to start the next one.

Overall, Rachel was grateful for the role that self-help books had played in her journey of self-improvement. She knew that she still had a long way to go, but she felt more confident and capable than ever before, and she was excited to see what the future held.

In the same manner you can also improve your life using self-help books.

ONE

"DEEP WORK" BY CAL NEWPORT

"Deep Work" is a book written by Cal Newport that argues for the importance of "deep work" - the ability to focus without distraction on a cognitively demanding task - in today's digital age. Newport argues that the ability to do deep work is becoming increasingly rare, as the constant distractions of the internet and social media have made it more difficult to focus and achieve flow. However, he also argues that the ability to do deep work is becoming increasingly valuable, as it allows individuals to produce high-quality work in a shorter amount of time and to differentiate themselves in a crowded and competitive job market.

One of the key themes of the book is the idea that the ability to do deep work is becoming increasingly rare. Newport writes, "The Deep Work Hypothesis: The ability to perform deep work is becoming increasingly rare at exactly the same time it is becoming increasingly valuable in our economy." He argues that the constant distractions of the internet and social media have made it more difficult for people to focus and achieve flow, leading to a decline in the ability to do deep work.

Another key theme of the book is the idea that the ability to do deep work is becoming increasingly valuable. Newport writes, "As the economy shifts towards a greater reliance on knowledge work and away from physical labor, those who possess the skills necessary to thrive in this new economy will see their options and opportunities expand." He argues that the ability to do deep work allows individuals to produce high-quality work in a shorter amount of time and to differentiate themselves in a crowded and competitive job market.

In addition to discussing the importance of deep work, Newport also offers practical strategies for how to cultivate this ability. He advises the reader to establish clear goals, to use their time effectively, and to minimize distractions. He also discusses the importance of creating a conducive environment for deep work, such as by designing a workspace that is free from distractions or by scheduling dedicated blocks of time for deep work.

Overall, "Deep Work" is a thought-provoking and practical guide to the importance of focus and concentration in today's digital age. Newport's ideas are based on his own experiences and observations, as well as research in the fields of psychology and productivity. Whether you're a student, a professional, or just looking to increase your productivity and achieve your goals, this book offers valuable insights and practical strategies that can help you cultivate the ability to do deep work and excel in your chosen field.

TWO

"As a Man Thinketh" by James Allen

"As a Man Thinketh" is a book written by James Allen and first published in 1902. The book is a philosophical treatise that explores the idea that our thoughts shape our reality and that we have the power to control our own destinies through the power of our thoughts. Allen argues that our thoughts are the driving force behind our actions and that by controlling our thoughts, we can shape our circumstances and achieve success and happiness.

One of the key themes of the book is the idea that our thoughts shape our reality. Allen writes, "As a man thinketh in his heart, so is he." He argues that our thoughts are the driving force behind our actions and that by controlling our thoughts, we can shape our circumstances and achieve success and happiness. This idea is central to Allen's philosophy, which emphasizes the power of positive thinking and the importance of focusing on what we want rather than what we fear.

Another key theme of the book is the idea that we have the power to control our own destinies. Allen writes, "The soul attracts that which it secretly harbors; that which it loves, and also that which it fears." He argues that by focusing our thoughts on what we want and cultivating positive attitudes, we can shape our lives and achieve our goals. He also advises the reader to "cultivate the habit of dwelling on the good, the beautiful, and the positive" in order to attract positive experiences and outcomes.

In addition to discussing the power of thoughts and the importance of positive thinking, Allen also addresses the role of action in achieving our goals. He writes, "The dreamers are the saviors of the world." He argues that it is not enough to simply dream and think positively - we must also take action in order to bring our dreams to fruition. He advises the reader to "translate [their] thoughts into acts" in order to achieve their goals and create the life they want.

Overall, "As a Man Thinketh" is a thought-provoking and inspiring book that explores the idea that our thoughts shape our reality and that we have the power to control our own destinies through the power of our thoughts. Allen's ideas are based on his own observations and experiences, and have inspired generations of readers to cultivate positive attitudes and take control of their lives. Whether you're seeking inspiration, guidance, or just looking to improve your life and achieve your goals, this book offers valuable insights and practical strategies that can help you create the life you want.

THREE

"HOW TO WIN FRIENDS & INFLUENCE PEOPLE" BY DALE CARNEGIE

"How to Win Friends and Influence People" is a self-help book written by Dale Carnegie and first published in 1936. The book teaches the reader about the power of positive relationships and how to build them through effective communication and interpersonal skills. Carnegie's ideas are based on his own experiences and observations, as well as the experiences of others.

One of the key themes of the book is the importance of treating others with kindness and respect. Carnegie writes, "You can make more friends in two months by becoming interested in other people than you can in two years by trying to get other people interested in you." This idea is at the heart of Carnegie's philosophy, which emphasizes the value of building genuine connections with others through empathy and understanding.

Another key theme of the book is the importance of communication in building and maintaining positive relationships. Carnegie advises the reader to "let the other person feel that the idea is his or hers," and to "talk about your own mistakes before criticizing the other person." These strategies help to create an open and non-threatening environment, which is essential for building trust and fostering good relationships.

At the heart of Carnegie's philosophy is the idea that positive relationships are the key to success in all areas of life. He argues that by treating others with kindness, respect, and understanding, we can build strong connections that can help us achieve our goals. Carnegie writes, "You can make more friends in two months by becoming interested in other people than you can in two years by trying to get other people interested in you." This idea is central to his approach, which emphasizes the importance of empathy and understanding in building genuine connections with others.

Effective communication is another key theme of the book. Carnegie advises the reader to "let the other person feel that the idea is his or hers," and to "talk about your own mistakes before criticizing the other person." These strategies help to create an open and non-threatening environment, which is essential for building trust and fostering good relationships. Carnegie also stresses the importance of being a good listener, writing, "To be interesting, be interested." By genuinely listening to others and showing an interest in what they have to say, we demonstrate our respect for them and build stronger connections.

In addition to these core ideas, Carnegie also discusses a wide range of other topics related to building and maintaining positive relationships. He offers advice on how to handle difficult people, how to negotiate effectively, and how to persuade others to see things your way. He also explores the importance of self-improvement and personal growth, and offers practical tips for developing confidence and self-esteem.

Overall, "How to Win Friends and Influence People" is a comprehensive and practical guide to building and maintaining positive relationships. Carnegie's ideas are timeless and continue to be relevant today, as the importance of strong interpersonal skills has only grown in an increasingly interconnected world. Whether you're looking to improve your relationships with colleagues, friends, or loved ones, this book offers valuable insights and practical strategies that can help you achieve your goals.

Take aways from Each Chapter-:

FUNDAMENTAL TECHNIQUES IN HANDLING PEOPLE

If you want to gather honey, don't kick over the beehive

--> In any situation, we should not criticize anyone, because we can hurt anyone by doing so and the person will not show any kind of interest further while talking to us and not I have not said never correct anyone you can but there are some techniques to do so.

Don't judge anyone, to whom you are not up to the mark to judge.

Don't criticize anyone, they are just what you would be under similar circumstances. And also Sharp criticisms and rebukes almost invariably end in futility. Always remember that any fool can criticize, condemn and complain, and most fools; But it takes character and self-control to be understanding and forgiving.

A great man shows his greatness by the way he treats little men.

Always try to figure out "Why they do, what they do." Remember that God himself does not judge a man until the end of his days.

Principle 1--> Don't Criticize, condemn or complain.

2. The big Secret of Dealing with people

-->There is only one way under high heaven to get anyone to do anything, making the other person want to do it. "The desire is important."

We should every time try to appreciate the other person and try to compliment the other person and it will help us to be in their good books.

Everybody likes a compliment, the deepest principle in human nature is the craving to be appreciated. A study shows that people go insane when they feel that they are not appreciated and are not important to anyone or in society. The way to develop the best that is in a person is by appreciation and encouragement. There is nothing a person needs so much as nourishment for his/her self-esteem. There is a difference b/w flattery and appreciation remember that in long run, flattery will do you more harm than good, and also don't be afraid of enemies who attack you; but be afraid of the friends who flatter you. Flatter is telling the other person precisely what he thinks of himself. Honest appreciation got results where criticism and ridicule failed. Every man I meet is my superior in some; In that, I learn from him. Always be hearty in your approbation and lavish in your praise.

Principle 2--> Give honest and sincere appreciation.

3. He who can do this has the whole world with him. He who can't walk a lonely way.

--> If you wanna bait a fish, you will never bait the hook with your favorite food instead you will bait what is liked by the fish. Every person is interested in what he wants. So the only way on the earth to influence other people is to talk about what they want and show them how to get it. First, arouse in the other person an eager want. He who can do this has the whole world with him, he who can't walk a lonely way. If there is anyone's secret to success, it lies in the ability to get the other person's point of view and see things from that person's angle as well as from your own.

Principle 3--> Arouse in the other person an eager want.

SIX WAYS TO MAKE PEOPLE LIKE YOU

1. Do this and you'll be welcome anywhere

-->If other people think that you are interested in them while talking, they will enjoy talking to you and will be feeling that you are important. You can make more friends in two months by becoming interested in other people than you can in two years by trying to get other people interested in you. It is the individual who is not interested in his fellow men who has the greatest difficulties in life and provides the most significant injury to others. It is from among such individuals that all human failures spring. You have to be interested in people if you want to be a successful influencer. One can win the attention and time and cooperation of even the most sought-after people by becoming genuinely interested in them. If we want to make friends, let's put ourselves out to do things for other people-things that require time, energy, unselfishness, and thoughtfulness. Also talking about ourselves, we are interested in others when they are interested in us.

Principle 1--> Become genuinely interested in other people.

2. A simple way to make a good first impression.

--> It is not important to wear expensive clothes on your body to make a good impression, remember that the expression one wears on one's face is far more important than the clothes one wears on one's back. The best expression for the first visit is a smile because Action speaks louder than words, and a smile says," I like you. You make me happy. I am glad to see you.". People who smile, tend to manage, teach and sell more effectively, and raise happier children. There's far more information than a frown. That's why encouragement is a much more effective device than punishment. You must have a good time meeting people if you expect them to have a good time meeting you. The action seems to follow feeling, but action and feeling go together; and by regulating the action, which is under the more direct control of the will, we can indirectly regulate the feeling which is not. There is nothing either good or bad but thinking makes it so. Don't fear being misunderstood and don't waste a minute thinking about your enemies, for nobody needs a smile so much as those who have none left to give!

Principle 2--> Smile.

3. If you don't do this, You are headed for trouble.

The best word that a person enjoys while listening to others talk is the person's name. An average person is more interested in his or her name than in all the other names on the earth put together. People are so proud of their names that they strive to perpetuate them at any cost.

Principle 3--> Remember that a person's name is to that person the sweetest and most important sound in any language.

4. An easy way to become a good conversationalist

--> All the people want an interested listener, so one could expand his/her ego and tell about where they had been. There is no mystery about successful business intercourse exclusive attention to the person who is speaking to you is very important. Nothing else is so flattering as that. Listening is just important nones home life as in the business world. Most people prefer good listeners over good talkers, but the ability to listen seems rarer than almost any other good trait. Be an attentive listener, to be interesting, be interested. Ask questions, that the other person will enjoy answering. People you are talking to are a hundred times more interested in themselves and their wants and problems than they are in you and your problems.

Principle 4--> Be a good listener. Encourage others to talk about themselves.

How to interest people.

--> The royal road to a person's heart is to talk about the things he or she treasures the most. If you talk about yourselves to others, they will not feel interested but if you speak to them about their kind of interests, they will feel far more interested.

Principle 5--> Talk in terms of the other person's interest.

How to make people like you Instantly

--> Make others feel that they are important, the greatest desire in a human being is the craving for appreciation. Treat others the way you wanted to be treated. Be hearty in your approbation and lavish in your praise. Almost everyone considers themselves important, very IMPORTANT. Let other people feel "YOU ARE IMPORTANT". Talk to people about themselves and they will listen to you for hours.

Principle 6--> Make the other person feel important-and do it sincerely.

HOW TO WIN PEOPLE TO YOUR WAY OF THINKING

You can't win an argument

--> Remember that there is only one way under high heaven to get the best out of an argument and that is to avoid it. Avoid it as you would avoid rattlesnakes and earthquakes. If you argue and rankle and contradict, you may achieve a victory sometimes; but it will be an empty victory because you will never get your opponent's goodwill. You may be right, dead right, as you speed along in your argument; but as far as changing another's mind is concerned, you will probably be just as futile as if you were wrong. Misunderstanding is never ended by an argument but by tact, diplomacy, conciliation, and a sympathetic desire to see the other person's viewpoint. When one yells, the other should listen because when two people yell, there is no communication, just noise, and bad vibrations.

Principle 1--> The only way to get the best out of an argument is to avoid it.

A sure way of making Enemies and how to avoid it

--> Never tell people that they are wrong. You can't teach a man anything but can only help him to find it within himself. You will never get in trouble by admitting that you are wrong. A lot of damage can be done if you tell a person straight out that he or she is wrong. You only succeed in stripping that person of self-dignity and making yourself an unwelcome part of any discussion. Judge people by their principles- not by your own. Always be diplomatic as it will help you gain your point, don't argue with anyone; don't tell them they are wrong, and don't get them stirred up. USE A LITTLE DIPLOMACY.

Principle 2 -> Show respect for the other person's opinion. Never say, "you're wrong".

If you're Wrong, Admit it

--> There is a certain degree of satisfaction in having the courage to admit one's errors. It not only clears the air of guilt and defensiveness but often helps solve the problem created by the error. If you are wrong admit it quickly and emphatically. When we are right let's try to win people gently and tactfully to our way of thinking, and when we are wrong- and that will be surprisingly often if we are honest with ourselves- let's admit our mistakes quickly and with enthusiasm. Not only will that technique. By fighting you never get enough but by yelling you get more than you expected.

Principle 3 -> If you are wrong, admit it quickly and emphatically.

A drop of honey

--> A drop of honey catches more honey than a gallon of gall. The sun can make you take off your coat more quickly than the wind; and kindliness, friendly approach, and appreciation can make people change their minds more readily than all the bluster and storming in the world.

Principle 4 -> Begin in a friendly way.

The Secret of Socrates

--> In talking with people, don't begin by discussing the things on which you differ. Begin by emphasizing-and keep on emphasizing-the things on which you agree. Keep emphasizing, if possible, that you both striving for the end and that your only difference is of the method and not of purpose. The more "Yeses" we can, at the very outset, induce, the more likely we are to succeed in capturing the attention of our ultimate proposal. It doesn't pay to argue, that it is much more profitable and much more interesting to look at things from the other person's viewpoint and try to get that person to say 'yes, yes."Socratic methods," was based upon getting a 'yes, yes' response. "He who treads softly goes far."

Principle 5 --> Get the other person to say "yes, yes" immediately,

The Safety Value in Handling Complaints

--> Most people trying to win others to their way of thinking do too much talking themselves. Let the other people talk themselves out. They know more about their business and the problems that you do. So ask them questions. Let them tell you a few things.

"If you want enemies, excel your friends; but if you want friends, let your friends excel you."

Principle 6--> Let the other person do a great deal of talking.

How to Get Cooperation

--> Isn't it wiser to make suggestions and let the other person think out the conclusion? No one likes to feel that he or she is being sold something or told to do a thing. We prefer to feel that we are buying of our own accord or acting on our ideas. We like to be consulted about our wishes, our and wants, our thoughts. "In every work of genius we recognize our own rejected thoughts; they come back to us with a certain alienated majesty."

Principle 7--> Let the other person feel that the idea is his or hers.

A Formula That Will Work Wonders for You

Remember that other people may be wrong. But they don't think so. Try honestly to put yourself in his place. "by becoming interested in the cause, we are less likely to dislike the effect. " "Stop a minute," "Success in dealing with people depends on a sympathetic grasp of the other person's viewpoint." "Cooperativeness in conversion is achieved when you show that you consider the other person's ideas and feelings as important as you own." Seeing things through another person's eyes may ease the tension when the personal problem becomes overwhelming.

Principle 8--> Try honestly to see things from the other person's point of view.

What Everybody Wants

"I don't blame you one iota for feeling as you do. If I were you I would undoubtedly feel just as you do." "There, but for the grace of God, go I"

PRINCIPLE 9. Be sympathetic with the other person's ideas and desires.

An Appeal That Everybody Likes

The ones that sound good are the real ones. You may be right. Nothing will work in all cases and nothing will work with all cases-and nothing will work with all people. If you are satisfied with the results you are now getting, why change? If you are not satisfied, why not experiment?

PRINCIPLE 10. Appeal to the nobler motives

The Movies Do It. TV Does It. Why Don't You Do It?

This is the day of dramatization, merely stating a truth isn't enough. The truth has to be made vivid, interesting, and dramatic. The movies do it. Television does it. And you will have to do it if you want attention.

PRINCIPLE 11. Dramatize your ideas.

When Nothing Else Works, Try This

"The way to get things done is to stimulate competition, I do not mean in a sordid, money-getting way, but in the desire to excel." The desire to excel! The challenge! Throwing down the gauntlet! An infallible way of appealing to people of spirit. "All men have fears, but the brave put down their fears and go forward, something to death, but always to victory." The one major factor that motivated people was the work itself.

PRINCIPLE 12. Throw down a challenge

FOUR

"55 QUESTIONS TO ASK YOURSELF, ACROSS 8 DIMENSIONS FOR A NEW YOU!" BY MANOJ CHENTHAMARAKSHAN

Introduction-:

This book by Manoj Chenthamarakshan helps you to identify your potential and boost your self-esteem by asking 55 questions about the same. Questioning yourself is one of the powerful ways to unlock some hidden thing about yourself that you never knew.

Self-Discovery-:

Who am I?

How do I view myself? Positive or negative?

Who are your top three role models?

What are those qualities that you admire in them?

What are your top 3 strengths?

What are the top obstacles that you overcome? How did you do so?

What do you love doing? (In terms of career and passion)

What do you like about yourself?

What makes you lose track of time?

If money was abundant in your life, what would you do?

What if that one thing that you continue doing even if you have all the riches in the world?

What completes you as a person?

What are you complimented for usually?

Goal Questions-:

What fulfills me as an individual?

What skills do I have to achieve this goal?

Why else would I need to achieve this goal?

When do I want to achieve this?

What would happen if I achieve this goal?

How would your surroundings change when you achieve this goal?

What would you see, hear and feel once you achieve this goal?

How would you remind yourself to stay on track during the journey?

Belief and Value Questions-:

What do you stand for?

What irritates you the most?

What are you ready to fight for?

What does a successful person mean to you?

What is the difference between the present you and the success you?

What is holding me back to take action?

What do you need to change mentally?

How would you do them?

What habits do you need to change?

How would you change the habits you need to change?

What is your favorite animal and why?

If you should describe yourself in a single word, what would that be?

Opportunity Questions-:

What could you do to change this situation?

What resources do you have currently to achieve your goals?

What else could you do to reach this goal?

Whom can you get help from?

Which option do you think would be the effective one?

What do you think is required to speed up this process?

Action Questions-:

What do I want to achieve in 6 months?

What do I want to achieve in 3 months?

What do I want to achieve in 1 month?

What do I want to achieve this week?

What are the resources that I need to stay on track?
What would keep me from taking action? And how do I deal with it?
Habit Questions-:
What new habits should I follow to achieve this goal? List them.
What would remind you to stick with the plan?
Accountability Questions-:
Whom will you associate with?
Whose help is required for you?
Whom will you call when you feel down or low?
Who is your coach?
Celebration questions-:
What were your biggest achievements this year?
How would you celebrate once you achieve this goal?
What is the milestone celebration?
Whom would you share this victory with once you have achieved it?

FIVE

"THE ART OF PUBLIC SPEAKING" BY DALE CARNEGIE

"The Art of Public Speaking" is a book written by Dale Carnegie and first published in 1915. The book is a comprehensive guide to effective public speaking and covers a wide range of topics, including how to prepare and deliver a speech, how to overcome stage fright, and how to connect with an audience.

One of the key themes of the book is the importance of preparation in public speaking. Carnegie advises the reader to "know your subject thoroughly" and to "plan your talk." He also emphasizes the importance of practicing, writing, "The only way to get the best of an argument is to avoid it." By thoroughly preparing for a speech and practicing it beforehand, we can increase our confidence and reduce the risk of making mistakes or getting flustered during the actual presentation.

Another key theme of the book is the importance of connecting with the audience. Carnegie writes, "The only way to get the best of an argument is to avoid it." He advises the speaker to "begin with a pleasing personality" and to "use your own natural style." By adopting a friendly and engaging demeanor and speaking in a way that feels authentic and natural, we can more easily build a rapport with the audience and engage them in the content of our speech.

In addition to discussing the importance of preparation and connecting with the audience, Carnegie also addresses the role of emotion in public speaking. He writes, "Emotions are a great help in the delivery of a speech, but they must be used with care." Carnegie advises the speaker to use emotion to enhance their message, rather than letting it overwhelm them or distract them from the content of their speech.

Overall, "The Art of Public Speaking" is a comprehensive and practical guide to effective public speaking. Carnegie's ideas are based on his own experiences and observations, as well as the experiences of others, and are timeless in their relevance. Whether you're a seasoned speaker or just starting out, this book offers valuable insights and practical strategies that can help you improve your public speaking skills and deliver more engaging and impactful presentations.

Takeaways of Each Chapter-:

Acquiring confidence before an audience

Face the audience as frequently as you can 'PRACTICE'. Be confident enough before your audience. Don't attempt to look or act great. Make a connection with your audience. Be well prepared with your topic. Be confident, not over-confident. Make the audience feel a relationship with you. Don't be haste, it shows a lack of control. Make your audience think like you. Be both mentally and physically prepared.

The sin of monotony

Monotony reveals our limitations, it's poverty both in life and speech. The variety gives pleasure to both audience & speaker. Use grammatical tools to remove monotony. Try to add force, pull, feelings, emotions, etc to your speech emotionally.

Efficiency through emphasis and subordination

Emphasis can be laid down not by rules but by feelings. Don't emphasize on random things, remember the gun that scatters too much, doesn't bag the bird. Emphasis only on important ideas. The big word in your speech should be mountain peaks, others the submerged streambeds. Emphasis is a matter of contrast & compassion, deliver the word differently which is to be emphasized. The force applied should not only be physical but also mental.

Efficiency through a change of pitch

Every change in the thought demands a change in the voice pitch. The necessity for changing pitch is so self-evident that it should be grasped and applied immediately. By sudden change of pitch during speeches, the speaker achieves great emphasis and suggests the gravity of the question raised.

Efficiency through a change of pace

Change in the rate of speaking is very important while speaking to increase the emphasis and power. It also helps prevent monotony. Thought rather than rules must govern you while speaking.

Pause and power

Pause, in public speech is not mere silence, its silence is made designedly eloquent. Speaker may be effective despite stumbling, but never because of it. Pause either before or after important words.

Advantages of pause-:

Enables the mind of the speaker to gather his forces before delivering the final volley.

Pause prepares the mind of the audience to receive your message.

It creates effective suspense.

Pausing after an important idea gives it time to penetrate.

Thought is more significant than punctuation. It must guide you in your pauses.

Efficiency through Inflection

Inflection- rise and fall of your voice while speaking.

The effectiveness of the speech is directly proportional to the change of inflection. It's not so much what you say, as how you say it.

Concentration in delivery

Attention is the microscope of the mental eye. While speaking one sentence, don't think of the sentence to follow. Speak, don't anticipate. Divide your attention and you divide your power. To concentrate is simply to attend to one thing, and nothing else.

Force

Force arises from conviction. Live with your subject until you are convinced of its importance.

Force can be acquired by Ideas, Feeling about the subject, Wording, and Delivery.

Your choice of words can also be helpful. Begin with words that demand attention. End with words that deserve distinction.

Feeling and Enthusiasm

The speeches that will live have been charged with emotional forces. The speaker who would speak efficiently must develop the power to arouse feeling. People will remember not what you said but how you made them feel. Don't let your words say one thing, and your voice and attitude another.

Fluency through preparation

In all matters, before beginning diligent preparation should be made. Fluency is almost entirely a matter of preparation. Readiness is preparedness. They are most ready and are best prepared. The vocabulary you have enlarged by study, the ease in speaking you have developed by practice.

Voice

There is something in that voice, that reaches the innermost recess of the spirit. Your throat must be free of strain during speech. You should speak correctly, not loudly to be heard at a distance. Don't speak too long without renewing your breath. Never attempt to force your voice, when hoarse. Never speak with a bad throat.

Voice Charm

A cheerful temper joined with innocence will make beauty attractive, knowledge delightful and wit good-natured. The joyous tones are the bright tones. If you want to possess voice charm, cultivate a deep, sincere sympathy for mankind.

Distinctness and precision of utterance

Essential factors for Precision utterance are- Articulation, Accentuation, and Enunciation.

How you utter, the clarity & precision in your word is very important for public speech. "Unclear Seriousness" is always undesired. Don't try to mutate someone. Learn to utter clearly. Your words should not slur.

Reason for bad articulation- ignorance of the elemental sounds, failure to differentiate some sounds, slovenly, inactive will.

Accentuation- is simply pronunciation, which can be improved by using a dictionary and listening.

Enunciation- 'clear expression', wrong enunciation gives the wrong sound to a word. Improved by the habitual utterance of words.

The truth about gesture

"outward expression of an inward condition". The gesture must be born, not built. Depends on personal good taste. Expression of your thoughts in actions. Includes all physical movements. Your audience should not follow your gesture but thoughts related to it, any gesture that merely calls attention to itself is bad. The gesture should be born of the movements. Avoid monotony, and use variety. Don't use useless movements. It should be simultaneous to the words. Posture is also very important.

Methods of delivery

The methods to choose depends upon circumstances & audience.

Reading from the manuscript- This is just an essay and not speaking. Done when language should be more precise, your facts more accurate and you are known other qualities. Avoid it!

Committing the written speech & speaking from memory- Best plays & speeches are not written, they are rewritten. Jotting down a complete speech may help eliminate errors. New speakers may not sound good. Use your mind for jotting down the points.

Speaking from notes- The best method for beginners. Using as few notes as possible will be helpful. Use them only if compiled to do so.

Extemporaneous speech- Most difficult but ideal method. You need more control over knowledge and language. Make notes on your brain instead of a paper.

Joint method of Delivery- A personal favorite technique for speaking. Can take some crucial notes and others extempore.

Thought and Reserve Power

You should have reserved words in your mind to speak perfectly. Don't speak without having ideas. Reserve power is the cream knowledge you got from observation, reading, experience, feeling, and thoughts.

Reserve power can be attained by seeing & think (Experience) or Reading(others' experience).

Think about the subject and its content yourself, reading will be very helpful & work as a stimulus to thought. Approach each subject with an open mind i.e. read both +ive and –ive aspects.

"Cherish your ability to think creatively and thinking can only be improved once you have knowledge and opinions of different people."

Subject and Preparation

Knowledge is organized information. Use your all senses to gather information as a public speaker. Read great speeches whenever you get time, speech preparation is not a one-day task.

Subject Choice- Arbitrary Choice; Development from thought and reading;

Development from thought and reading is more suitable as it grips the speaker. If by chance you choose 'Arbitrary Choice', then you can focus on managing time wisely by allocating a fixed one to each part. Short speeches are more liked. Keep in mind the very important part. Get your facts prepared beforehand with accuracy.

Reading books easily:-

Got to index;

Search for usable and important topics;

Read them making notes;

REMEMBER- more speeches have been spoiled by half-hearted preparation than lack of talent.

Make your own method of note-taking by considering many speakers. After note taking writes/develop your speech with the main focus on expression rather than thoughts.

Revision is a must- imagine being in front of an audience.

Give the title to your speech at the end, it should be fresh, short, suited to the subject, and likely to excite interest.

Influencing by exposition

Telling the real meaning of the subject. It builds a foundation of facts for later arguments. The exposition gives- clearness, precision, accuracy, unity, truth, and necessity. Exposition directly deals with the meaning or intent of its subjects instead of appearance.

Influencing by Description

To describe is to call up a picture in the mind of the listener. Exposition deals with general. Description with particular. The description should be mainly by suggestion. Learn the power of words to make scenery. Choose only significant details, eliminating others. Be very sure and confident about your viewpoint. Add emotion to your description. One thing in life calls for another.

Influencing by Narration

Narration includes anecdotes, biographical facts, and narration of events in general. Begin anecdote with witty sentences. Biographical facts make your speech a practical one. The narration of events in general makes your speech interesting.

Influencing by Suggestion

Most of our opinions and actions are not based upon conscious reasoning but are the result of suggestions. Try to dominate the thoughts of your listeners.

Suggestion affect as-:

We naturally respect authority;

Least line of resistance;

Influenced by embarrassment.

Making suggestions effective-:

As a speaker be confident, its the mother of conviction;

Try to be an authority;

State some examples;

Use of figurative language.

Influencing by Argument

The argument includes- Building up an argument and breaking down an argument.

Arguments can be made strong by:

Knowing the question under discussion;

Evidence;

Reasoning.

Influencing by Persuasion

Persuasion is the most effective way of influencing. Know your audience. Study your audience. The successful pleader must convert his arguments into terms of his listeners' advantage. Feel your topic deeply.

Influencing the crowd

The feeling of the crowd is distinct. A sense of responsibility is lost in the crowd. The crowd always has a leader. The crowd can be controlled by attacking feeling, not logic. Appeal to the emotions. Have your audience seated compactly.

Riding the winged horse.

Imagination is a process of forming mental images.

1. Reproductive imagination- Imagining a previous experience. Includes visual image, auditory image, motor image, gustatory image, olfactory image, and tactile image.

2. Productive imagination- complete imagination.

Imagination in Public Speaking:-

Imaging in Speech- Preparation-;

Set the image of your audience;

Conceive your speech as a whole;

Image the language you will use.

Imaging in speech delivery-:

Reimage past emotions;

Reconstruct in the image the scenes you are to describe.

Image the objects in nature whose tone you delineate.

Growing your Vocabulary

Add words of value to your everyday stock-:

From the book- note habit;

From reference- book habit;

Use synonyms;

Discuss words with those who know them;

Search for best-suited words.

Memory training

A reliable memory is an invaluable possession for the speaker. Don't follow rote learning. Concentration is the first step of memorizing. Be attentive.

To memorize, be in a calm place.

Pick out essentials.

Associate your ideas.

Repetition.

Read thoughtfully aloud.

Write important.

Right thinking and personality.

The most valuable possession is personality. Develop a strong character. Your thought and mental attitude determine your failure & success.

After-dinner & another occasional speaking.

Study the occasion, and respect it. Occasional speeches include humor. Use short speeches.

Making conversation effective

The conversation has more power than the press and platform combined. Listen to another person. Choose a subject of general interest. Don't talk about yourself. Remain silent if you have nothing interesting.

SIX

"THE POWER OF YOUR SUBCONSCIOUS MIND" BY DR. JOSEPH MURPHY

"The Power of the Subconscious Mind" is a book written by Dr. Joseph Murphy that explores the concept of the subconscious mind and its role in shaping our lives. Murphy argues that the subconscious mind is a powerful force that can be harnessed to achieve success, happiness, and fulfillment. He offers practical advice and techniques for accessing and harnessing the power of the subconscious mind, including visualization, affirmations, and creative visualization.

One of the key themes of the book is the idea that the subconscious mind is a powerful force that can be harnessed to achieve our goals. Murphy writes, "The subconscious mind is the builder of your body and the maker of your circumstances, conditions, and environment." He argues that by accessing and harnessing the power of the subconscious mind, we can shape our circumstances and achieve success, happiness, and fulfillment.

Another key theme of the book is the idea that our thoughts and beliefs shape our reality. Murphy writes, "Your conscious and subconscious thoughts create your reality." He argues that by changing our thoughts and beliefs, we can change our circumstances and create the life we want. He advises the reader to "think and act upon the assumption that you are what you want to be" in order to attract positive experiences and outcomes.

In addition to discussing the power of the subconscious mind and the role of thoughts and beliefs in shaping our reality, Murphy also offers practical techniques for accessing and harnessing the power of the subconscious mind. These techniques include visualization, affirmations, and creative visualization, which can help the reader to focus their thoughts and manifest their goals.

Overall, "The Power of the Subconscious Mind" is a thought-provoking and inspiring book that explores the concept of the subconscious mind and its role in shaping our lives. Murphy's ideas are based on his own experiences and observations, as well as research in the fields of psychology and personal development. Whether you're seeking inspiration, guidance, or just looking to improve your life and achieve your goals, this book offers valuable insights and practical techniques that can help you access and harness the power of the subconscious mind.

SEVEN

"THE ALCHEMIST" BY PANLO COELHO

"The Alchemist" is a novel written by Paulo Coelho that tells the story of Santiago, a shepherd boy who embarks on a journey to find his personal legend and fulfill his dreams. Along the way, Santiago meets a series of characters who help him to understand the importance of following his heart and trusting in the power of the universe to guide him on his path. The novel is a fable that explores themes of self-discovery, personal growth, and the pursuit of one's dreams.

One of the key themes of the novel is the idea of personal legend - the belief that each person has a unique purpose or destiny that they are meant to fulfill. Santiago is guided on his journey by the belief in his personal legend, which he understands to be the purpose for which he was created. Throughout the novel, Santiago grapples with the idea of personal legend and learns to trust in the power of the universe to guide him on his path.

Another key theme of the novel is the idea of self-discovery and personal growth. Santiago's journey is one of self-discovery, as he learns to listen to his heart and trust in himself. Along the way, he encounters a series of challenges and obstacles that test his resolve and help him to grow as a person. Santiago learns to let go of his fears and doubts and to embrace his true self, and in doing so, he becomes more confident and self-aware.

In addition to exploring themes of personal legend and self-discovery, the novel also touches on the idea of the interconnectedness of all things. Santiago comes to understand that everything in the universe is connected and that each person is a part of something greater. This understanding helps him to find meaning and purpose in his journey and to trust in the power of the universe to guide him.

Overall, "The Alchemist" is a moving and inspiring novel that tells the story of Santiago, a shepherd boy who embarks on a journey to find his personal legend and fulfill his dreams. The novel is a fable that explores themes of self-discovery, personal growth, and the pursuit of one's dreams, and encourages the reader to follow their heart and trust in the power of the universe to guide them on their path.

EIGHT

"THE 7 HABITS OF HIGHLY EFFECTIVE PEOPLE" BY STEPHEN R. COVEY

"The 7 Habits of Highly Effective People" is a self-help book written by Stephen R. Covey that explores the habits and behaviors of highly effective individuals. The book is divided into two parts: "Private Victory" and "Public Victory." In the first part, Covey focuses on the habits and behaviours that lead to personal effectiveness and fulfillment, while in the second part, he discusses the habits and behaviors that lead to success in relationships and in the broader community.

One of the key themes of the book is the importance of personal responsibility. Covey argues that highly effective individuals take ownership of their lives and take responsibility for their actions and outcomes. He writes, "Private Victory precedes Public Victory. Self-mastery is the foundation of effective leadership." Covey advises the reader to "begin with the end in mind" and to "put first things first," in order to prioritize their goals and take control of their lives.

Another key theme of the book is the importance of effective communication and interpersonal skills. Covey argues that highly effective individuals are able to communicate effectively and build strong relationships with others. He advises the reader to "seek first to understand, then to be understood," and to "synergize," in order to build trust and cooperation with others. Covey also emphasizes the importance of being proactive, rather than reactive, in order to achieve success. He writes, "Proactive people are responsible for their own lives. They are responsive to the needs and concerns of others and make things happen."

Overall, "The 7 Habits of Highly Effective People" is a comprehensive guide to personal and professional effectiveness, offering practical advice and strategies for improving one's habits and behaviors in order to achieve success in all areas of life.

NINE

"Man's Search for Meaning" by Viktor Frankl

"Man's Search for Meaning" is a book written by Viktor Frankl, a Holocaust survivor and psychotherapist. The book is a memoir of Frankl's experiences in concentration camps during World War II, and it is also a treatise on the importance of meaning and purpose in life. Frankl argues that the search for meaning is a fundamental human need and that even in the most difficult circumstances, it is possible to find meaning and purpose in life.

One of the key themes of the book is the idea that the search for meaning is a fundamental human need. Frankl writes, "The question of meaning is the primary question for man." He argues that as human beings, we have a deep-seated need to find meaning and purpose in life, and that this need is what gives us the strength to endure even the most difficult circumstances. Frankl's own experiences in the concentration camps, where he saw countless people suffer and die, led him to believe that the search for meaning is what gives us the resilience and strength to survive even the most extreme conditions.

Another key theme of the book is the idea that it is possible to find meaning and purpose in life even in the most difficult circumstances. Frankl writes, "Everything can be taken from a man but one thing: the last of the human freedoms - to choose one's attitude in any given set of circumstances, to choose one's own way." He argues that even in the face of suffering and adversity, we have the power to choose our attitude and to find meaning and purpose in life. Frankl's own experience in the concentration camps, where he witnessed people who were able to find meaning and purpose even in the most extreme conditions, helped him to develop his theory of logotherapy, which is a form of psychotherapy that focuses on helping people to find meaning and purpose in life.

In addition to these themes, "Man's Search for Meaning" also explores the importance of love and relationships in our lives. Frankl writes that love is a powerful force that can give us the strength to endure even the most difficult circumstances, and that it is through our relationships with others that we are able to find meaning and purpose in life.

Overall, "Man's Search for Meaning" is a poignant and thought-provoking book that explores the human need for meaning and purpose, and offers a powerful message of hope and resilience in the face of suffering and adversity.

TEN

"Awaken the Giant Within" by Tony Robbins

"Awaken the Giant Within" is a self-help book written by Tony Robbins that explores the idea that we all have the power to take control of our lives and achieve our goals. The book is divided into four parts: "The Driving Force," "The Invisible Forces," "The Path," and "The Ultimate Success Formula." In each part, Robbins discusses a different aspect of personal development and offers practical advice and techniques for how to achieve success and fulfillment in life.

One of the key themes of the book is the idea that we all have the power to take control of our lives and achieve our goals. Robbins argues that our thoughts and beliefs shape our reality and that by changing our thoughts and beliefs, we can change our lives. He writes, "The first step in changing your life is to change the way you think about things." Robbins advises the reader to "believe in themselves" and to "take control of their thoughts" in order to achieve their goals.

Another key theme of the book is the importance of taking action in order to achieve our goals. Robbins argues that simply thinking about our goals is not enough - we must also take action in order to bring them to fruition. He writes, "The only thing that stands between you and your dream is the will to try and the belief that it is actually possible." Robbins advises the reader to "take massive action" in order to make their dreams a reality.

In addition to discussing the power of thoughts and the importance of taking action, the book also covers a wide range of topics related to personal development, including goal-setting, time management, communication skills, and relationships. Robbins offers practical advice and techniques for how to overcome obstacles and achieve success and fulfillment in all areas of life.

Overall, "Awaken the Giant Within" is an inspiring and practical guide to personal development and achievement. Robbins' ideas are based on his own experiences and observations, as well as research in the fields of psychology and personal development. Whether you're seeking inspiration, guidance, or just looking to improve your life and achieve your goals, this book offers valuable insights and practical techniques that can help you to awaken the giant within and take control of your life.

ELEVEN

"The Power of Now" by Eckhart Tolle

"The Power of Now" is a self-help book written by Eckhart Tolle that explores the concept of living in the present moment and the benefits of doing so. Tolle argues that our thoughts and emotions often keep us trapped in the past or the future, causing us to miss out on the present moment. He offers practical advice and techniques for how to let go of our thoughts and emotions and to focus on the present moment, in order to find peace, happiness, and fulfillment.

One of the key themes of the book is the idea that living in the present moment is the key to happiness and fulfillment. Tolle writes, "The present moment is the only place where life exists." He argues that by focusing on the present moment, we can let go of our thoughts and emotions, which often keep us trapped in the past or the future, and find peace and contentment in the present. Tolle advises the reader to "be present" and to "let go of the mind" in order to find inner peace and happiness.

Another key theme of the book is the idea that our thoughts and emotions often keep us trapped in the past or the future. Tolle writes, "The past has no power to stop you from being present now. Only your grievance about the past can do that." He argues that by letting go of our thoughts and emotions, we can free ourselves from the grip of the past and the future, and find happiness and fulfillment in the present. Tolle advises the reader to "accept the present moment" and to "let go of the mind" in order to break free from the cycle of thoughts and emotions that keep us trapped in the past and the future.

In addition to discussing the concept of living in the present moment and the benefits of doing so, the book also covers a wide range of topics related to personal development and spiritual growth. Tolle offers practical advice and techniques for how to find inner peace.

Overall, "The Power of Now" is a thought-provoking and insightful book that explores the idea that living in the present moment is the key to happiness and fulfillment. Tolle's ideas are based on his own experiences and observations, as well as his studies in spirituality and personal development. Whether you're seeking inner peace, happiness, or just looking to improve your life, this book offers valuable insights and practical techniques that can help you to find greater peace and fulfillment by living in the present moment.

TWELVE

"THINK AND GROW RICH" BY NAPOLEON HILL

"Think and Grow Rich" is a self-help book written by Napoleon Hill that explores the idea that we can achieve success and wealth by harnessing the power of our thoughts and beliefs. Hill argues that our thoughts and beliefs shape our reality and that by focusing on success and wealth, we can attract these things into our lives. The book is based on Hill's interviews with successful individuals, including Andrew Carnegie and Henry Ford, and it offers practical advice and techniques for how to achieve success and wealth.

One of the key themes of the book is the idea that our thoughts and beliefs shape our reality. Hill writes, "Whatever the mind of man can conceive and believe, it can achieve." He argues that by focusing our thoughts and beliefs on success and wealth, we can attract these things into our lives. Hill advises the reader to "fix in their mind the exact amount of money they desire" and to "determine unswervingly to attain it" in order to achieve their goals.

Another key theme of the book is the importance of taking action in order to achieve success and wealth. Hill writes, "Action is the real measure of intelligence." He argues that simply thinking about our goals is not enough - we must also take action in order to bring them to fruition. Hill advises the reader to "take action on their plans" and to "persevere until they succeed" in order to achieve their goals.

In addition to discussing the power of thoughts and the importance of action, the book also covers a wide range of topics related to personal development and success. Hill offers practical advice and techniques for how to overcome obstacles, set and achieve goals, and build a successful mindset.

Overall, "Think and Grow Rich" is an inspiring and practical guide to achieving success and wealth. Hill's ideas are based on his own research and interviews with successful individuals, and they offer valuable insights and practical techniques for how to achieve your goals and build a successful life. Whether you're seeking inspiration, guidance, or just looking to improve your life and achieve your goals, this book offers valuable insights and practical strategies that can help you achieve your dreams.

THIRTEEN

"The Art of Happiness" by the Dalai Lama and Howard C. Cutler

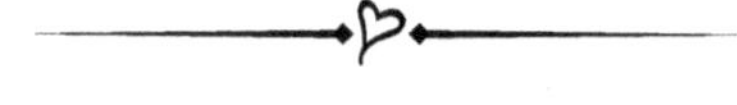

"The Art of Happiness" is a book written by the Dalai Lama and Howard C. Cutler that explores the concept of happiness and offers practical advice for how to cultivate happiness in our lives. The book is based on a series of conversations between the Dalai Lama and Cutler, in which the Dalai Lama shares his teachings and insights on happiness, and Cutler asks questions and seeks clarification. The book covers a wide range of topics related to happiness, including mindfulness, compassion, relationships, and spirituality.

One of the key themes of the book is the idea that happiness is a choice and that we have the power to cultivate happiness in our lives. The Dalai Lama writes, "Happiness is not something ready made. It comes from your own actions." He argues that by focusing on positive emotions, cultivating compassion, and living in the present moment, we can find happiness in our lives. The Dalai Lama advises the reader to "cultivate a positive state of mind" and to "cultivate compassion" in order to cultivate happiness.

Another key theme of the book is the importance of mindfulness and living in the present moment. The Dalai Lama argues that our thoughts and emotions often keep us trapped in the past or the future, causing us to miss out on the present moment. He advises the reader to "pay attention to the present moment" and to "be present" in order to cultivate happiness and find peace and contentment.

In addition to discussing the concept of happiness and the importance of mindfulness, the book also covers a wide range of topics related to personal development and spiritual growth. The Dalai Lama offers practical advice and techniques for how to cultivate compassion, build meaningful relationships, and find meaning and purpose in life.

Overall, "The Art of Happiness" is an inspiring and practical guide to cultivating happiness in our lives. The book is based on the teachings and insights of the Dalai Lama, and it offers valuable advice and techniques for how to cultivate a positive state of mind, cultivate compassion, and find happiness in our lives. Whether you're seeking inspiration, guidance, or just looking to improve your life and find happiness, this book offers valuable insights and practical strategies that can help you cultivate happiness and find peace and contentment in your life.

FOURTEEN

"THE SUBTLE ART OF NOT GIVING A F*CK" BY MARK MANSON

"The Subtle Art of Not Giving a F*ck" is a self-help book written by Mark Manson that explores the idea that we should focus on the things that matter and not waste our time and energy on things that don't. Manson argues that our culture often encourages us to worry about things that are not important, and that this leads to stress, anxiety, and unhappiness. He offers practical advice and techniques for how to prioritize our values and focus on the things that are truly important, in order to find happiness and fulfillment.

One of the key themes of the book is the idea that we should focus on the things that matter and not waste our time and energy on things that don't. Manson writes, "The key to happiness, it seems, is finding out what is actually worth giving a f*ck about and what isn't." He argues that by prioritizing our values and focusing on the things that are truly important, we can find happiness and fulfillment. Manson advises the reader to "identify their values" and to "focus on the things that matter" in order to find happiness and fulfillment.

Another key theme of the book is the importance of accepting reality and letting go of the things that we cannot control. Manson writes, "One of the most fundamental skills we can learn in life is learning how to let go." He argues that by accepting reality and letting go of the things that we cannot control, we can find peace and contentment. Manson advises the reader to "accept reality" and to "let go of the things that don't matter" in order to find happiness and fulfillment.

In addition to discussing the importance of focusing on the things that matter and accepting reality, the book also covers a wide range of topics related to personal development and happiness. Manson offers practical advice and techniques for how to cultivate a positive mindset, develop healthy relationships, and live a fulfilling life. He also addresses common challenges and obstacles that people face in their pursuit of happiness, and provides strategies for overcoming these challenges.

Overall, "The Subtle Art of Not Giving a F*ck" is a thought-provoking and practical guide to finding happiness and fulfillment by focusing on the things that matter and letting go of the things that don't. Whether you're struggling with stress and anxiety, or simply looking to improve your life and find more meaning and purpose, this book offers valuable insights and strategies that can help you on your journey.

FIFTEEN

"TOOLS OF TITANS" BY TIM FERRISS

"Tools of Titans" is a self-help book written by Tim Ferriss that explores the habits and routines of highly successful individuals. The book is based on Ferriss' interviews with over 200 successful people, including entrepreneurs, athletes, celebrities, and writers, and it offers practical advice and techniques for how to achieve success and fulfillment in life. The book is divided into three parts: "Healthy," "Wealthy," and "Wise," and it covers a wide range of topics related to personal development, productivity, and success.

One of the key themes of the book is the idea that successful individuals have specific habits and routines that contribute to their success. Ferriss writes, "The small daily habits of successful people are what set them apart from the rest." He argues that by adopting the habits and routines of successful individuals, we can improve our own lives and achieve success. Ferriss advises the reader to "identify the habits of successful people" and to "adopt those habits" in order to achieve success.

Another key theme of the book is the importance of personal growth and development. Ferriss writes, "The pursuit of personal growth is never-ending." He argues that successful individuals are constantly seeking to improve themselves and to learn new things, and that this is an essential part of achieving success. Ferriss advises the reader to "seek personal growth" and to "never stop learning" in order to achieve success.

In addition to discussing the habits and routines of successful individuals and the importance of personal growth, the book also covers a wide range of topics related to productivity, success, and happiness. Ferriss offers practical advice and techniques for how to set and achieve goals, manage time and energy, and cultivate a positive mindset.

Overall, "Tools of Titans" is an inspiring and practical guide to achieving success and fulfillment in life. The book is based on Ferriss' interviews with over 200 successful people, and it offers valuable insights and practical techniques for how to adopt the habits and routines of successful individuals and to pursue personal growth and development. Whether you're seeking inspiration, guidance, or just looking to improve your life and achieve your goals, this book offers valuable insights and practical strategies that can help you achieve success and fulfillment. In addition, the book's wide range of topics related to personal development, productivity, and success make it a valuable resource for anyone looking to improve various aspects of their life.

SIXTEEN

"THE 48 LAWS OF POWER" BY ROBERT GREENE

"The 48 Laws of Power" is a book written by Robert Greene that explores the concept of power and offers practical advice for how to acquire and maintain power in various aspects of life. The book is divided into 48 chapters, each of which covers a different law of power, and it is based on Greene's research into the lives and tactics of historical figures who have wielded power, such as Machiavelli and Sun Tzu. The book covers a wide range of topics related to power, including leadership, persuasion, manipulation, and strategy.

One of the key themes of the book is the idea that power is a central part of human nature and that we all have the potential to acquire and wield power. Greene writes, "Power is a force that can be harnessed and channeled, and it is the central driving force in the universe." He argues that by understanding the laws of power and applying them in our own lives, we can acquire and maintain power in various aspects of life. Greene advises the reader to "study the laws of power" and to "apply them in their own life" in order to acquire and maintain power.

Another key theme of the book is the idea that power is often acquired and maintained through manipulation, deception, and strategy. Greene argues that successful individuals often use these tactics to gain and maintain power, and he advises the reader to do the same. He writes, "Manipulation, deception, and strategy are all essential tools in the pursuit of power." Greene advises the reader to "employ manipulation and deception" and to "use strategy" in order to acquire and maintain power.

In addition to discussing the concept of power and the tactics used to acquire and maintain it, the book also covers a wide range of topics related to personal development and leadership. Greene offers practical advice and techniques for how to build influence, persuade others, and navigate complex social situations.

Overall, "The 48 Laws of Power" is a provocative and thought-provoking guide to acquiring and maintaining power in various aspects of life. The book is based on Greene's research into the lives and tactics of historical figures who have wielded power, and it offers valuable insights and practical techniques for how to acquire and maintain power in your own life. Whether you're seeking inspiration, guidance, or just looking to improve your life and achieve your goals, this book offers valuable insights and practical strategies that can help you acquire and maintain power in various aspects of life. However, it is important to note that the tactics and strategies recommended in the book may not align with everyone's personal values and beliefs, and readers should carefully consider the potential consequences of applying these techniques in their own lives. The book also emphasizes the importance of understanding the context in which power is exercised, and advises the reader to carefully consider the long-term consequences of their actions. Overall, "The 48 Laws of Power" is a valuable resource for anyone seeking to improve their understanding of power and to acquire and maintain power in various aspects of life.

SEVENTEEN

"The Success Principles" by Jack Canfield

"The Success Principles" is a self-help book written by Jack Canfield that explores the principles and practices of successful individuals and offers practical advice for how to achieve success in various aspects of life. The book is divided into 64 chapters, each of which covers a different principle of success, and it covers a wide range of topics related to personal development, goal-setting, and achievement.

One of the key themes of the book is the idea that successful individuals have specific habits and practices that contribute to their success. Canfield writes, "Successful people do things differently from the rest of us. They think differently, they act differently, and they get different results." He argues that by adopting the habits and practices of successful individuals, we can improve our own lives and achieve success. Canfield advises the reader to "identify the habits and practices of successful people" and to "adopt those habits and practices" in order to achieve success.

Another key theme of the book is the importance of setting and achieving goals. Canfield writes, "Goals are the roadmap to success." He argues that successful individuals set clear and specific goals and work consistently towards achieving them, and he advises the reader to do the same. Canfield offers practical advice and techniques for how to set and achieve goals, including tips for setting SMART goals (specific, measurable, achievable, relevant, and time-bound) and for creating a plan of action to achieve those goals.

In addition to discussing the habits and practices of successful individuals and the importance of goal-setting, the book also covers a wide range of topics related to personal development, leadership, and achievement. Canfield offers practical advice and techniques for how to develop a positive mindset, build confidence, and overcome obstacles and challenges.

Overall, "The Success Principles" is an inspiring and practical guide to achieving success in various aspects of life. The book is based on Canfield's extensive research and experience as a success coach and motivational speaker, and it offers valuable insights and practical strategies that can help you achieve your goals and improve your life. Whether you're seeking inspiration, guidance, or just looking to improve your life and achieve your goals, this book offers valuable insights and practical strategies that can help you on your journey.

EIGHTEEN

"The Secret" by Rhonda Byrne

"The Secret" is a self-help book written by Rhonda Byrne that explores the concept of the law of attraction and how it can be used to manifest success, happiness, and abundance in life. The book is based on the idea that our thoughts and feelings have the power to attract events, experiences, and people into our lives, and that by focusing on positive thoughts and feelings, we can manifest our desires. The book covers a wide range of topics related to personal development and goal-setting, including the power of positive thinking, the importance of gratitude, and the role of visualization in manifesting our goals.

One of the key themes of the book is the idea that our thoughts and feelings have the power to shape our reality. Byrne writes, "The law of attraction is forming your entire life experience and it is doing that through your thoughts." She argues that by focusing on positive thoughts and feelings, we can attract positive experiences and outcomes into our lives. Byrne advises the reader to "focus on positive thoughts and feelings" and to "visualize their desires" in order to manifest their goals.

Another key theme of the book is the importance of gratitude. Byrne argues that expressing gratitude helps to shift our focus from lack and negativity to abundance and positivity, and that this can help to attract more of what we want into our lives. She advises the reader to "focus on gratitude" and to "count their blessings" in order to manifest their goals.

In addition to discussing the law of attraction and the power of positive thinking and gratitude, the book also covers a wide range of topics related to personal development and goal-setting. Byrne offers practical advice and techniques for how to set and achieve goals, build self-confidence, and cultivate a positive mindset.

Overall, "The Secret" is an inspiring and thought-provoking guide to using the law of attraction to manifest success, happiness, and abundance in life. The book is based on the idea that our thoughts and feelings have the power to shape our reality, and it offers practical advice and techniques for how to harness that power and manifest our goals. Whether you're seeking inspiration, guidance, or just looking to improve your life and achieve your goals, this book offers valuable insights and practical strategies that can help you manifest your desires.

NINETEEN

"The Four Hour Work Week" by Timothy Ferriss

"The Four Hour Work Week" is a self-help book written by Timothy Ferriss that explores the concept of lifestyle design and offers practical advice for how to achieve more freedom and flexibility in your life. The book is based on the idea that traditional models of work and success are outdated and that it is possible to achieve financial and personal success without working long hours or sacrificing your personal life. The book covers a wide range of topics related to personal development, productivity, and entrepreneurship, including the importance of setting and achieving goals, the power of automation and delegation, and the value of personal branding.

One of the key themes of the book is the idea that it is possible to achieve financial and personal success without working long hours or sacrificing your personal life. Ferriss writes, "The New Rich (NR) are those who abandon the deferred-life plan and create luxury lifestyles in the present using the currency of the New Rich: time and mobility." He argues that by adopting the strategies and tactics of the New Rich, we can achieve more freedom and flexibility in our lives. Ferriss advises the reader to "adopt the strategies and tactics of the New Rich" and to "build a business that allows you to live the lifestyle you want" in order to achieve more freedom and flexibility.

Another key theme of the book is the importance of setting and achieving goals. Ferriss argues that successful individuals set clear and specific goals and work consistently towards achieving them, and he advises the reader to do the same. He writes, "The question you need to ask yourself is not 'What do I want to achieve?' but 'What do I want my life to look like?'" Ferriss offers practical advice and techniques for how to set and achieve goals, including tips for setting SMART goals (specific, measurable, achievable, relevant, and time-bound) and for creating a plan of action to achieve those goals.

In addition to discussing the concept of lifestyle design and the importance of goal-setting, the book also covers a wide range of topics related to personal development, productivity, and entrepreneurship. Ferriss offers practical advice and techniques for how to automate and delegate tasks, build a personal brand, and achieve financial success.

Overall, "The Four Hour Work Week" is an inspiring and practical guide to achieving more freedom and flexibility in your life. The book is based on the idea that traditional models of work and success are outdated and that it is possible to achieve financial and personal success on your own terms. Ferriss offers a range of strategies and tactics for how to build a business or career that allows you to live the lifestyle you want, and he emphasizes the importance of setting and achieving goals, automating and delegating tasks, and building a personal brand. While some of the ideas and techniques outlined in the book may not be applicable to everyone, the book offers valuable insights and practical strategies that can help readers achieve more freedom and flexibility in their lives.

TWENTY

"Eat That Frog!: 21 Great Ways to Stop Procrastinating and Get More Done in Less Time" by Brian Tracy

"Eat That Frog!" is a self-help book written by Brian Tracy that explores the concept of productivity and offers practical advice for how to overcome procrastination and get more done in less time. The book is based on the idea that we all have tasks and responsibilities that we don't want to do, but that by tackling these "frogs" first thing in the morning, we can set the tone for a productive day and make progress towards our goals. The book covers a wide range of topics related to productivity, including time management, goal-setting, and overcoming procrastination.

One of the key themes of the book is the importance of setting and achieving goals. Tracy writes, "The first step in overcoming procrastination is to set clear, specific, and measurable goals for yourself." He argues that successful individuals set clear and specific goals and work consistently towards achieving them, and he advises the reader to do the same. Tracy offers practical advice and techniques for how to set and achieve goals, including tips for setting SMART goals (specific, measurable, achievable, relevant, and time-bound) and for creating a plan of action to achieve those goals.

Another key theme of the book is the importance of prioritization and time management. Tracy argues that successful individuals are able to prioritize their tasks and manage their time effectively, and he advises the reader to do the same. He writes, "The key to getting more done in less time is to identify your most important tasks and work on them first." Tracy offers practical advice and techniques for how to prioritize tasks and manage your time effectively, including tips for creating a to-do list and for using time-management tools and techniques.

In addition to discussing the importance of goal-setting and time management, the book also covers a wide range of topics related to overcoming procrastination and increasing productivity. Tracy offers practical advice and techniques for how to overcome procrastination and increase your productivity, such as setting deadlines, breaking tasks down into smaller steps, and using motivation and accountability to help you stay on track. He also emphasizes the importance of taking care of yourself and your physical and mental well-being in order to be more productive, and he offers strategies for managing stress, staying focused, and avoiding distractions.

Overall, "Eat That Frog!" is a practical and straightforward guide to overcoming procrastination and increasing productivity. Tracy offers a range of strategies and techniques that can help readers get more done in less time, and he emphasizes the importance of setting and achieving goals, prioritizing tasks, and taking care of yourself in order to be more productive. Whether you're looking for inspiration, guidance, or just looking to improve your productivity, this book offers valuable insights and practical strategies that can help you get more done in less time.

TWENTY-ONE

"12 Rules for Life: An Antidote to Chaos" by Jordan Peterson

"12 Rules for Life: An Antidote to Chaos" is a self-help book written by Canadian clinical psychologist and psychology professor Jordan B. Peterson. The book has been a bestseller, with its central theme being the importance of taking personal responsibility in order to live a fulfilling life.

One of the key ideas in the book is the importance of facing one's problems and challenges rather than avoiding them. As Peterson writes: "What you do every day matters more than what you do once in a while. It's better to do something difficult that you have to do than to do something easy that you want to do." This message is in line with the first rule of the book, "Stand up straight with your shoulders back," which advises readers to take on the responsibilities of life with confidence and integrity.

Another key concept in the book is the idea of the "hero's journey," which is the idea that each person must go through a process of self-discovery and personal growth in order to achieve their full potential. Peterson writes: "The adventure of life is about becoming the person you were designed to be. It is about discovering who you are and what you are capable of, and then learning how to use that knowledge to live well."

In addition to discussing these overarching themes, the book also addresses a wide range of specific issues, such as the importance of work, the dangers of tribalism and ideology, the value of forgiveness and compassion, and the role of storytelling in shaping our lives.

Throughout the book, Peterson weaves in personal anecdotes and stories from his own life and his work as a clinical psychologist, as well as insights from literature, philosophy, and religion. He also frequently draws on the work of other thinkers and writers, including Carl Jung, Friedrich Nietzsche, and Aleksandr Solzhenitsyn.

Overall, "12 Rules for Life" is a thought-provoking and thought-provoking book that encourages readers to take a proactive approach to their lives and to strive for personal growth and fulfillment. As Peterson writes: "There is meaning to be found in life. It is not an easy thing to find, but it is worth the effort. And the effort is not in vain, because the meaning of life is not something that you find, it is something that you create."

TWENTY-TWO

"THE ATOMIC HABITS" BY JAMES CLEAR

"Atomic Habits" is a self-help book written by James Clear, a writer, speaker, and entrepreneur. The book focuses on the importance of small, incremental changes in behavior, known as "atomic habits," in achieving long-term success.

Clear argues that small habits, when compounded over time, can lead to significant improvements in an individual's life. He writes: "Habits are the compound interest of self-improvement. The same way that money multiplies through compound interest, the effects of your habits multiply as you repeat them. They seem to make little difference on any given day and yet the impact they deliver over the months and years can be enormous."

To help readers build and maintain good habits, Clear offers a four-step process known as the "Habit Loop": cue, craving, response, and reward. He suggests identifying the cue that triggers a particular behavior, understanding the craving that drives it, and finding a positive response that will satisfy that craving and lead to a reward.

Clear also emphasizes the importance of creating a positive environment for habit formation, such as setting clear goals, minimizing distractions, and making it easy to engage in good habits. He writes: "Your environment is the most powerful force shaping your behavior. It's the invisible hand that guides your actions."

Throughout the book, Clear offers practical strategies and tips for building good habits and breaking bad ones, as well as real-life examples of individuals who have successfully used these techniques to make positive changes in their lives.

One strategy that Clear recommends for building good habits is to make them attractive, by adding something that you enjoy to the start of a new habit. He writes: "The more attractive an activity is, the more likely it is that you will do it. So if you want to start a new habit, make it attractive in some way."

Clear also advises readers to make their habits obvious, by setting clear reminders and cues to trigger the desired behavior. He writes: "The more obvious a cue is, the more likely it is to be effective. To make your habits more obvious, you can use implementation intentions, which are simple if-then statements that link a specific trigger to a desired action."

In addition to these strategies, Clear also stresses the importance of making habits easy to do, by minimizing the number of steps required to complete them and making them convenient and accessible. He writes: "The more effort a habit requires, the less likely it is to be performed. To make a habit easier to do, you can reduce the number of steps required to complete it, make the habit more convenient, or increase the chances that you will encounter a cue for the habit."

Overall, "Atomic Habits" is a helpful and insightful guide to building good habits and improving one's life through small, consistent changes in behavior. As Clear writes: "You are what you repeatedly do. Excellence, then, is not an act, but a habit."

TWENTY-THREE

"Attitude is Everything" by Jeff Keller

"Attitude is Everything" is a self-help book written by Jeff Keller, a motivational speaker and business coach. The book focuses on the power of positive thinking and the role that attitude plays in an individual's success and happiness.

Keller introduces the concept of "The Attitude Triangle," which is made up of thoughts, emotions, and behaviors, and argues that our thoughts play a crucial role in shaping our attitudes and ultimately our lives. He writes: "Your thoughts are the most powerful force in your life. They have the power to lift you up or bring you down. They have the power to make you or break you."

To help readers develop a positive attitude, Keller offers strategies such as setting goals, visualizing success, and focusing on the present moment. He also emphasizes the importance of taking control of one's thoughts and choosing to focus on the positive. He writes: "You have the power to choose your thoughts. You can choose to focus on the positive or the negative. You can choose to be a glass-half-full or glass-half-empty person."

Keller also discusses the value of developing a growth mindset, which is the belief that one's abilities and potential can be developed and improved through effort and learning. He writes: "A growth mindset is the belief that you have the power to change, to grow, to learn, to improve. It is the belief that no matter what has happened in the past, you have the power to shape your future."

Throughout the book, Keller offers practical advice and real-life examples to illustrate the power of a positive attitude and its impact on an individual's life. He writes: "Your attitude is everything. It determines how you feel, how you act, and how you react to the world around you. It is the single most important factor in your life."

Overall, "Attitude is Everything" is a motivating and inspiring guide to developing a positive attitude and improving one's life through the power of positive thinking. As Keller writes: "Your attitude is a choice. Choose wisely."

TWENTY-FOUR

"You Can" by George Matthew Adams

"You Can" is a self-help book written by George Matthew Adams, a journalist and motivational speaker. The book is focused on the power of positive thinking and the role that belief plays in achieving success and happiness.

Adams begins the book by discussing the importance of having a clear sense of purpose in life. He writes: "The most successful people in life are those who have a definite purpose. They know what they want, and they go after it with all the energy and enthusiasm of which they are capable."

According to Adams, having a positive attitude is crucial to achieving success and realizing one's potential. He writes: "Belief is the most important factor in success. Without belief, you can accomplish nothing. With belief, you can accomplish anything."

To help readers develop a positive attitude and overcome obstacles, Adams offers a number of strategies and techniques, such as setting goals, visualizing success, and focusing on the present moment. He also emphasizes the importance of taking action and being persistent in the face of challenges. He writes: "Action is the key to success. Without action, nothing can be accomplished. With action, everything is possible."

Throughout the book, Adams offers practical advice and real-life examples to illustrate the power of positive thinking and the impact it can have on an individual's life. He writes: "You can do anything you want to do, be anything you want to be, if you will only believe in yourself and go after your dreams with all your heart."

Overall, "You Can" is a motivating and inspiring guide to developing a positive attitude and achieving success through the power of positive thinking. As Adams writes: "Believe in yourself and all that you are. Know that there is something inside you that is greater than any obstacle."

TWENTY-FIVE

"Life's Amazing Secrets" by Gaur Gopal Das

"Life's Amazing Secrets" is a self-help book written by Gaur Gopal Das, a spiritual leader and motivational speaker. The book is focused on the importance of finding inner peace and happiness through spiritual growth and self-discovery.

Das begins the book by discussing the concept of "inner wealth," which he defines as the peace and happiness that come from within. He writes: "Inner wealth is not about accumulating material possessions or external achievements. It is about finding contentment and fulfillment within ourselves, regardless of our circumstances."

According to Das, the key to inner wealth is self-awareness and understanding one's true nature. He writes: "To live a fulfilling life, it is essential that we understand our true nature and purpose. When we align ourselves with our true self, we experience inner peace and happiness."

To help readers achieve inner wealth and self-awareness, Das offers a number of strategies and techniques, such as meditation, mindfulness, and living in the present moment. He also emphasizes the importance of developing positive relationships and letting go of negative emotions. He writes: "Positive relationships are a source of joy and fulfillment. They enrich our lives and bring meaning to our existence. On the other hand, negative relationships drain us of energy and happiness."

Throughout the book, Das offers practical advice and spiritual insights to help readers find inner peace and happiness. He writes: "Life's amazing secrets are within us, waiting to be discovered. When we awaken to our true nature and purpose, we tap into an infinite source of joy, love, and inner peace."

Overall, "Life's Amazing Secrets" is a thought-provoking and inspiring guide to finding inner peace and happiness through spiritual growth and self-discovery. As Das writes: "The journey to inner wealth begins with self-awareness and understanding our true nature. When we align ourselves with our true selves, we tap into an infinite source of joy, love, and inner peace."

TWENTY-SIX

"Just as You Are: A Teen's Guide to Self-Acceptance and Lasting Self-Esteem" by Dr. Elizabeth Berger

"Just as You Are: A Teen's Guide to Self-Acceptance and Lasting Self-Esteem" is a self-help book written specifically for adolescents struggling with self-esteem issues. The author, Dr. Elizabeth Berger, is a child and adolescent psychiatrist with over 25 years of experience working with young people. In the book, she offers practical advice and strategies for improving self-esteem and developing a more positive self-image.

One of the key themes of the book is the importance of self-acceptance. Dr. Berger argues that self-acceptance is the foundation of healthy self-esteem, and that teens who are able to accept themselves as they are are better able to cope with the challenges and stresses of adolescence. She provides practical tips for cultivating self-acceptance, such as learning to recognize and challenge negative self-talk, and finding ways to celebrate and appreciate one's own unique qualities and strengths.

Another key theme of the book is the idea that self-esteem is not a fixed trait, but rather something that can be developed and strengthened over time. Dr. Berger provides a number of techniques and exercises for building self-esteem, including setting and achieving goals, practicing self-care, and seeking out positive relationships and social support.

Throughout the book, Dr. Berger emphasizes the importance of seeking out help when needed, and encourages teens to speak with a trusted adult, such as a parent, teacher, or counselor, if they are struggling with self-esteem issues. She also encourages teens to be patient with themselves and to recognize that building self-esteem is a process that takes time and effort.

In summary, "Just as You Are: A Teen's Guide to Self-Acceptance and Lasting Self-Esteem" is a valuable resource for adolescents looking to improve their self-esteem and build a more positive self-image. With its practical advice and strategies, it provides a roadmap for cultivating self-acceptance, setting and achieving goals, and building a strong foundation of self-esteem that will serve teens well throughout their lives.

TWENTY-SEVEN

"The 7 Habits of Highly Effective Teens" by Sean Covey

"The 7 Habits of Highly Effective Teens" is a self-help book written by Sean Covey, the son of Stephen Covey, author of the best-selling "The 7 Habits of Highly Effective People." In this book, Sean Covey adapts his father's principles for a teenage audience, offering practical advice for how adolescents can develop the habits that lead to personal effectiveness and success.

One of the key habits discussed in the book is the habit of proactivity. Covey defines proactivity as "the ability to take initiative and to make things happen, rather than simply reacting to events." He argues that proactive teens are more likely to be successful and fulfilled, as they are able to take charge of their own lives rather than being passive bystanders. Covey suggests a number of strategies for developing proactivity, such as setting goals, taking initiative, and being responsible for one's own actions.

Another key habit discussed in the book is the habit of prioritization, or the ability to focus on what is most important and to allocate one's time and energy accordingly. Covey emphasizes the importance of setting clear goals and priorities, and advises teens to be mindful of the long-term consequences of their actions. He also advises teens to be proactive in managing their time and to avoid procrastination, which he sees as a major barrier to personal effectiveness.

A third key habit discussed in the book is the habit of effective communication. Covey argues that effective communication is essential for building and maintaining positive relationships, and he provides tips and techniques for improving communication skills, such as listening actively, expressing oneself clearly and assertively, and managing conflict.

Throughout the book, Covey emphasizes the importance of self-reflection and personal growth, and he encourages teens to take the time to think about their values, goals, and priorities. He also stresses the importance of seeking out positive role models and mentors, and of seeking help when needed.

In summary, "The 7 Habits of Highly Effective Teens" is a valuable resource for adolescents looking to develop the habits that lead to personal effectiveness and success. With its practical advice and strategies, it provides a roadmap for cultivating proactivity, prioritization, and effective communication, and for cultivating a mindset of continuous personal growth and improvement.

TWENTY-EIGHT
"Grit" by Angela Duckworth

Grit is a book by Angela Duckworth that explores the idea that grit – defined as a combination of passion and persistence – is a better predictor of success than talent or intelligence. Duckworth argues that grit is something that can be developed and nurtured, and that it is a key factor in achieving long-term goals.

One key idea in the book is the concept of "deliberate practice," which refers to the idea that it takes a lot of hard work and focused effort to get good at something. According to Duckworth, this kind of practice involves setting specific, challenging goals, getting immediate feedback on performance, and concentrating as hard as possible. She cites research showing that it takes about 10 years or 10,000 hours of deliberate practice to become an expert in a particular field.

Another important concept in the book is the idea of "flow," which refers to the state of being completely absorbed in an activity. Duckworth argues that flow is important for developing grit, because it allows people to become so immersed in their work that they lose track of time and become highly productive. She suggests that people can increase their chances of entering a state of flow by setting challenging but achievable goals, and by finding work that is personally meaningful and engaging.

Duckworth also talks about the importance of having a growth mindset, or the belief that one's abilities can be developed through effort. She argues that people with a growth mindset are more likely to be gritty, because they are more open to challenges and more resilient in the face of setbacks.

One key takeaway from the book is that grit is not something that people are born with – it is something that can be developed. Duckworth suggests a number of ways that people can cultivate grit, including setting long-term goals, seeking out opportunities for deliberate practice, finding work that is personally meaningful, and surrounding oneself with supportive friends and family.

Here are a few quotations from the book that illustrate some of these ideas:

"Grit is passion and perseverance for very long-term goals. Grit is having stamina. Grit is sticking with your future, day in, day out, not just for the week, not just for the month, but for years, and working really hard to make that future a reality. Grit is living life like it's a marathon, not a sprint." (p. 3)

"Deliberate practice is purposeful and systematic. It requires that you identify the tasks or knowledge that are just out of your reach, strive to upgrade your performance, monitor your progress, and revise your approach as needed. Deliberate practice is not simply about putting in time; it's about seeking out opportunities for improvement, even when it's not easy." (p. 74)

"Flow is the state of being in the zone, of complete immersion in an activity. It is a state of great enjoyment, creativity, and productivity. When you are in flow, you are so focused on the task at hand that you lose all sense of time. You become one with your work." (p. 116)

"The growth mindset is the belief that you can grow and develop through effort. It is the opposite of a fixed mindset, which is the belief that your abilities are fixed and cannot be changed." (p. 120)

TWENTY-NINE
"Ikigai" by Hector Garcia and Francesc Miralles

Ikigai is a Japanese concept that roughly translates to "a reason for being." It refers to the idea that everyone has something that gives their life meaning and purpose, and that finding and pursuing this ikigai can lead to a happier and more fulfilling life.

In the book Ikigai: The Japanese Secret to a Long and Happy Life, authors Hector Garcia and Francesc Miralles explore the concept of ikigai and how it can be applied in modern life. They argue that ikigai is a combination of four elements: what you love, what you are good at, what the world needs, and what you can be paid for. Finding the intersection of these elements is key to discovering one's ikigai.

The authors also discuss the importance of maintaining a healthy lifestyle in order to nurture one's ikigai. This includes eating a healthy diet, staying active, getting enough sleep, and maintaining social connections. They argue that by taking care of one's physical and mental health, it becomes easier to find and pursue one's ikigai.

The book also explores the concept of "nekutai," or "the beauty of everyday life." This involves finding joy and meaning in the simple pleasures of daily life, such as spending time with loved ones, enjoying nature, and engaging in hobbies.

In addition to discussing the benefits of finding one's ikigai, the authors also provide practical tips and exercises for helping readers discover their own ikigai. This includes exploring one's interests, values, and strengths, and considering how they can be applied in a way that is meaningful and fulfilling.

Here are a few quotations from the book that illustrate some of these ideas:

"Ikigai is the reason for which we get up in the morning. It's the thing that gives us a reason to live, the thing that gives us joy and happiness." (p. 8)

"Ikigai is the intersection of what you are good at, what you love, what the world needs, and what you can be paid for. It's the place where your personal values and professional goals meet." (p. 21)

"Nekutai is the beauty of everyday life. It's about finding joy in the simple things, in the here and now. It's about living in the moment and enjoying the present." (p. 109)

"To find your ikigai, you need to explore your interests, values, and strengths. You need to consider what makes you happy and what you are good at. You need to think about what the world needs and what you can be paid for. And you need to consider how all of these elements intersect and how you can use them to create a meaningful and fulfilling life." (p. 183)

Thanks For Selecting This Book

"Thank you for selecting this book! As a reader, you are embarking on a journey of personal growth and self-improvement, and I am honored to be able to join you on this path.

These authors have dedicated their lives to helping others live to their full potential, and their words have inspired and guided millions of readers around the globe.

I hope that this book will serve as a valuable resource for you, providing guidance and inspiration as you work towards your goals and dreams. Thank you again for choosing this book, and I wish you all the best on your journey towards personal growth and self-improvement."

Follow Author on Social Media-:

Instagram- @krishivnegi

Twitter- @krshivnegi